The Tulip Sacrament

THE TULIP SACRAMENT

'ANNAH SOBELMAN

Wesleyan University Press
Published by University Press of New England
Hanover and London

Wesleyan University Press
Published by University Press of New England, Hanover, NH 03755
© 1995 by 'Annah Sobelman
All rights reserved
Printed in the United States of America   5   4   3   2   1
CIP data appear at the end of the book

The publisher gratefully acknowledges the support of Lannan Foundation in the publication of this book.

Contents

Acknowledgments / vii

Possible Margins of Error and Variation in the Matter Stream / xi

Meditation Bird / 1

Francis Ford Coppola's *Dracula* / 3

Bitter Bird / 5

I Am the *No* and the *Yes,* / 8

My Odessa / 10

Autumn Trees Cannot Fail to Promote the Talking / 12

Coming Home and the Mouth / 13

Cooking *Humantosh* / 17

The Hearts of Garlic Are Disappointed / 20

My Grandma and the Sack of Potatoes / 21

Snake / 25

Absolute Gravity, Time, the Clarinet / 28

Of Gravity, Menses, Tomatoes / 31

The White / 33

Coo Coo Ghost and the Leak / 35

Jesus and the Gray Sacrament / 36

When the Devoted Rats Come to Hide Themselves in My Breasts / 39

The Pigeons Have Decided Not to Wound the Sidewalks / 41

The Different Smokes on Top of the Roof / 43

Spring at the Cafe Figaro / 45

The Rats and the Dirt / 51

Spring at the Cafe Figaro 2 / 55

Inside the Cafe Lanterna di Vittorio / 64

Kissing the Flame and Yellow Tulips / 67

Quartet for Three Instruments / 69

The Tulip Sacrament / 72

Acknowledgments

Grateful acknowledgment is made to the editors of the following publications, in which some of these poems first appeared: *The Antioch Review*, "I am the *No* and the *Yes*," *The Colorado Review,* "Possible Margins of Error and Variation in the Matter Stream," "Jesus and the Gray Sacrament," and *Indiana Review*, "The Different Smokes on Top of the Roof."

The author would like to thank Toi Derricotte, Jocelyn Emerson, Jorie Graham, Robert Hass, Galway Kinnell and Sharon Olds, and especially Brenda Hillman.

for Sarah 1986–1993
and
for Herbert Ryan

Possible Margins of Error and Variation
in the Matter Stream

Since he can't find sleep anymore he paces on deck wondering

about what happened to him in the transporter stream when he was beamed up

    from the other location. *Occasionally very*
bright, and marathon soft

or stiff as frozen stars, even what they call the wastes

    are pretty. Matter

from the streamer might have been accidentally beamed aboard but why

    does he feel
so strange? *There's no margin*

for error, one atom off and poof you're gone,
    he'd initially argued not

    wanting
to be so unraveled

    and raveled back up again like that. *Tell*

me about your heart. And sure enough the dead body of his predecessor

lies there stiff
    like the slipknot of proof caught in

the broken fever of matter. *Could all this be equivalent to jazz?* Exploding

   the joints
of cerebral synapses, the old religion. *Does*

  the singeing of half-lives sing? He feels
his throat, his arm, his chest. Becomes thirstier than a bird. Ambles

past the pulsing big windows of

   space, stars silky with their trust-me implications, and when he asks the

computer stress reduction program it gives him in the accurate voice

  of the female *more*
birds beside the salty

  waves. Calm, calm,

he also intones as if to create a temporary home, *what* are *these variations*
  that keep whistling through

  the monster
blood so fast, so brave

if only I could catch catch catch them? Could he have imagined it,

they wonder? *Spatial relationships are all*
  distorted in the matter

stream. What marked his right arm like that? *Turned to fluorescent*

  confetti stored in fluctuating, windy

currency, detailed,

immense. Different, I tell you, than the sirens he was no longer groping

towards. *Matter*
matter matter, what

are these discrete
caches of light? The biofilter,

you see, could not distinguish between the molecules and the *something* which looked animal and even mythological

to him, part leopard part snake. *He pushed molecular dispersion way past the integrity*

point almost
just before the human

patterns began starting to degrade. They

did not expect it. What made him begin to start singing like that?

The Tulip Sacrament

Meditation Bird

Saying the word *homesick*
I don't mean the pigeons' light *coo*

cooing, heart branching out towards
yourself again, which is lemon

almost gurgling, pretty, its white
edges furled rolling *rrr's* like inimitable

French—or
pale and distant to

yourself, look how far you've come,
nice baby you also speak my

language, which is almost every pale
color of the City you can think of, pink,

lavender, blue, gray, mauve, white
iridescent and matte. But I do mean the pigeons'

wheezing *homing,*
homing as in negotiating constant change

on the brick window
between these apartments which is violet, or

bearing and raising many young,
reckless exquisite

attention, I adore you kindred beast
—devotion of the family—

on the shadow ledges
which is red. As well as

blood wound far from
home, healing

slowly wanting not to be in love—

which is the color garnet. And especially
my heart in those days

often in my hands, I gave to you
with fearless authority I now take it back

which is the color of sound squeezed
out through a slit blood-box—

Francis Ford Coppola's Dracula

At first there seems to be an argument about
the failure of nature. Count Dracula,
in the artifacts of his love has actually shriveled
around his own heart, which is now also a
remnant. His skin makes our skin revolt because it is severely
humiliated, though nevertheless supernaturally ruthless
with the absence of pity. His fingers twist
as if around his fingernails which are so
long and crooked they indicate physical pain. He
never even says *be my body* to each new woman
with his two extra teeth as he breaks the sexual tissue
of the neck. The blood
is not really the issue. There will be a
huge shadow moving behind the Count even when he's
not moving, as well as a necklace
of blue flames which will sweep into the women's bedrooms
and saturate them with its authority, or else the curling-
back snarl of the wolf. I am trying not
to judge Dracula or the woman
who falls in love with him again. At the moment
she gives herself I feel the warmth
and relax. He has not misled her.
I believe she knows what she will become.
There is that point in the movie when I decide that evil
is something that believes it cannot
be loved but decides to continue. I am sitting
in the theatre on Thanksgiving Day
in New York City pressing my shoes onto the floor,

pulling my black coat more tightly around my shoulders
because it is cold. I am thinking that
his body makes our body crawl because it is
in the process of limitless hurt.

Bitter Bird

When the voice said, *bodies
invested in deep water,* I thought of

him, quantum packet with his broad
back turned, still not knowing—(little

chunk of not totally
consistent language coming out,

my bright burned rooster, oh
Botticelli baby doll of the petit corn)—

who can see the obvious
menu, the over-compressed

consequences of his recent poems—
It was funny, touching,

really, to see the trucks all
standing there in line

by the side of the interstate
to be weighed on the way out of here.

I'm tired of the sticky
hot coffee that spills, couldn't

god have more imagination?
the sadness at the margins of the *no*

and the *no* and the *no*—my direct,
sidelong glance. I walked gingerly

across the highway,
barefoot, holding up my skirts—

trying to be the vessel
god would come to since I'd lost him,

especially since I'd lost him. There's
his stubby fingers looking concerned over there,

his stubbled, evening
shadow—the mosquitoes that pester

the flesh—the leeks, homely
and bulbous, cut at the roots, simmering

on the stove—this room I rented
for $20, it comes with air conditioning, a mirror,

and bed bowed,
slightly, bent as you now see it. Do you know

I'm tired of my own wide-
eyed surprise, the diminishing rings

within rings of the heavy
planets? The heart with its stone I have raised

underfoot, unreluctant, still slippery
bitterness, unattractive because it's so small,

small, lonely celibate hitchhiker—
you will forgive me the rockmoss,

these intensities. I understand the north,
finally, where you said you wanted to live—

chaste, ungenerous,
not to be bedded—extreme

with high glory winds. The heart passes
in then out of them,

rapture-bird, raucous mole,
oh piece of cut hair twisting between my hands—

I Am the No *and the* Yes,

a solid ghost and real, whose feet won't
glide like metal blades across

the body of lakes. Coughing up a solid spat
of yellow phlegm, I feel

you, guide
you with my fingers swelling towards a possible

door. Though I'll reel back
struck if I walk into a window as

if a heart of ice is shutting, the way the drums
can't find you sometimes when you dance, music

just sounds loud—the way
that bird once hurled itself for three months

against my window, sickening scary
thud when it stopped. *No,* I heard at every swimming

pool as I tried to peel the dead clothes
off my skin. But I've loved to dance against

the great gashed body of light, twisting
my hipbones in an intolerable tease. Outlaw *yes,* I am

the stick of ice melting
between your palms, I am the bird flinging

herself against the heartbreak glass. Say *no*
and feel the rods in my back stiffening—say *yes* and

see my hand pass
through the melting storms and gardens

of your shoulder, stick
of rib so holy I can close my hand over

it and pray. I am the *no*
and the *yes,* that friction you've been longing for.

My Odessa

No, maybe not a shadow,
my grandma Sarah would say, tired of seeing them everywhere, and

anyway she is what

she was in life, many faces, but, picture this, none of them moons exactly hanging
over mine. *Those forests were bright flesh inside*

night inside—All along they'd been
shrinking but it's not as if fright alone were seizing them. *You are the violin*

almost all of which cuts

into my shoulders, face, my two temples, and *Shtetls near Odessa*
the softness around me

stinks. It made me want to

shrink. For example, *pardon my italics,* or *I didn't mean to shiver*
this extra house, I attributed importantly to her

face inside Russia which felt large but also dwindling on top of her shoul-
    ders, her body
hung *over* my insides and then *inside* my

air as if she were the drawing
back of a prayer into the breath

of the wood because I thought I heard the bark of the singing trees

sigh. *It's not a curse,*

I said, explaining, as I know them, physics and science as a kind
of elliptical genetic dash and still softer

bits of strong violet
white stuff. *Beautiful horses were also in it, lights through the forest, you are my long*

*waist and shrinking
grandma neck.* In her mouth her dazzling shoulders and neck

lest anyone should break
them when they saw her. *Arguably,*

measurably, my body's been taking up less and less of the air. And to the thin white

skin notched with dark
brown fright hunching

where the birch were cut, my beloved old ones, also backing me up in
an important forest filled

with miles and miles of freight, I'm trying to
lean forward more than a

soft tongue inside a horse's bit since I think I can grow two, maybe three bodies

bigger across danger up
to the train-cutting-through-

them mountains—they're the Urals, horses firm—and then of course beyond

these mountains
since I think it's very

important to break the necks of soft houses with our shoulders—

Autumn Trees Cannot Fail to Promote the Talking

I feel scared and small again in the City of
young cat whimpering in her basket. Where are my
siblings? The smallness hid inside the skin. What started
it? My throat aches where the mother yanked
me by the neck to move my body. My voicebox trembles
on top of the world of *fear so many things.*
There are spasms of smallness that break
the far below yellow trees, but there is fervor of dancing
splitting open the belly of the earth, since it knows it can't be true. The sky
with its big furred back arched looked so convincing, in fact, as if I say
everything is possible. As if *earth is pomegranate
hide to all these seeds.* Last night I parted the sections of the fruit
and opened each one. As if by eating it I could
live there in *the parts are orphaned—to start speech
eat all the family.*

Coming Home and the Mouth

When I think about coming home, I think about the mouth.

The spirit pigeons stayed away from me almost right from the first, they recognized
    me, and all the noise,

the racket, the loud engines of the mouth! My furred
appetite linked to a genetically pliable stomach, spine and

    plastic bone marrow, meat

and warm sour milk breath blown out over everything, the tempting

City of bright *yes,* look
how long it takes to settle down

    between these moves, how fast the appetite begins to recover. I can't

exactly tell you what I do to be more at home—it's being more
patient with the air the way the cat hunches over the interesting mouse

corner—*you look
well, sleek and polished*

*with your canned gravied
meats,* the pigeons answer, *do you still want more?* The

    mouth almost always says *More, please.* A long, jagged

splintered thing to tear at, a smaller wriggly body to hunt, more
air, the comforting extracts of the dairy. Because eating

is letting the air agree with
you, you make your own place

    in it, wrestle with some kind of friction, smooth

onto anything rough. You eat so much that soon this decorator studio begins to look like you despite its wall-

papered pink and silver flowers and pastel coor-

    dinated rug you warn the cat not to claw

too much at, its metal lamps and paintings whose gesture must have been color matching, matching, so that when the owner

    returns she won't even recognize it—*bright conversion of space, digesting*

of the elements— so that even the City
shining down below, spread out far

in a landscape of geometries is looking for some feeling, some will

to help it change. Maybe even some mouth.

Though the pigeons do help, *it doesn't want to be married,* they say, *pity is
    what it's seeking—*

the interesting engines of the mouth

    —and when the pigeons say *you have to be willing to let the strange thing*

*in, you have to be willing to eat
it, I have dramatic skyline,*

you answer, *buildings like angular hearts, beasts, cats.* And the Zoloft doesn't

flatten you out but returns
you to your hunger, this blare of morning air, some combustion of oxygen

    and heat because when things become geometric

they're often more
eager to be consumed. I admire,

for example, the woman who stayed home on an important day to return

    to her center. I have breathed in the meat of airplanes
    and spit them out again, uncertain about their affects

and tasted the fat tongues of cats and pigeons, their notorious mixed
    wheezing squeals
as well as the moles my cat has killed, fresh and

red. Meanwhile, the cat, stretching her arms wide open, begins to

fly out over the City in her
famous cat imagination, her mouth

wide open. Out there wild on the stretch she says *if only cats*

had been given wings and mouths with aerial dimensions

    and I say *yes, that's kind of a shame. Cats with catwings would be great*

    for the cats but sad
    for the pigeons! Which doesn't

mean these sirens sending

up their machine squeaker voice high into the air where I'm sitting have to
   be acknowledged

   or ignored—*they're another body that wants to be eaten,*

wheeze the pigeons, *another spirit*
that wants to enter the mouth, genitalia

and blood. Even the angels, after all, with their strong feather voices which
   know nothing

of silt, liquid and the actual pleasure of
breathing. *Even this hunger with fur stripes*

and jellied sinuous bones with a lust for crouching, in fact for almost
   everything, I said—I suppose I was defending myself—

—even the word *devout,* whose name means *eat,* with a fierce silver fork

and prayer (language of the hungry
mouth) but elegant—*A convention of queer*

   space, reply the pigeons; I add *I am in heaven with a window!* Which is when

I said *home is where my jaw relaxes*—*I feed everybody*—

Cooking Humantosh

When I really wanted to
speak, she started making the interesting *humantosh* pastries. Birds

were coming out, too, not

speechless, starting to sing with even more dark whistle authority
since the *humantosh* tries to open up our mouths

when we get shut
in them. These birds were *black interrogatory*

upon black. These birds were *that throat sometimes inside pounding with the beaks*

by which in
Odessa my heart

inside winter harsh sounds gets stuck. By which she heard nightly

on the shores *bereaving,*
ferocious, steps, through what heart

inside winter would she have to sweep? To which, lighting candles,

triangular *humantosh*
fill up with prunes which talk about Esther speaking

loudly to her husband the king about the traitor Hamen in order to warn
   mad Israel
so they would not be without defense. Israel wouldn't stop

talking. Or *open up my old
stoves, heart of sweating plums.* This was to help me. *I'm sweeping*

in order to burn those bridges, she said, shoving out *bird
black soot,* and in fact, with my Jewish mouth, I'm cooking with

her right now in the old Odessa

oven which smells a lot like my
grandma's *sweeping fear arm out in the frost emigrant whoosh.* Were the prunes unlike

the rage? Is memory cooking in the

heating prune paste because she couldn't otherwise hold all her birds' hard
whistling? When I start speaking, she puts me

into the interesting
humantosh dough trying to get me to chew faster, birds especially

on her thick upper arms where she's sweeping methodically with such *husk-*

accent whisk since my childhood
also sometimes scared me. *I'm shoving living out toward*

plums of birds, she says, since there is still a lot of cooking to
be done above the thick emigrant sheets, meaning sleeping without

safety tears
things. Were the birds unlike the rage? Which

tore through her own feel slower? *Patter patter down the cobbled twilight*

18

*be quiet before
and after dark.* Which flew faster down her own nervous

roof? Or she'd say *sometimes I wondered about plucking*

*the rowdy plums off their
boughs, but still, if you can, believe in mouths and fortunate*

gambling. The violence is done to the plums so the ode to joy won't have to
    stumble down again
I hope, very much—*Oh mouth,*

she'd say, with the good heaviness coming up—*Oh heart,* I'd answer, also

coming up with her from the inside
of the stove since I wanted to get out and eat where the birds

and whisker chins
talk faster, full of tongues of *humantosh* and

talkative huge sighs, and since I wanted to also be more tasted—

The Hearts of Garlic Are Disappointed

At night the illness becomes
intense: the old empire nightie cut straight doesn't fit
your 'bosoms,' sprouting shelves of gray
hair eat your temples in a bleach. The collarbone becomes
ivory—teeth chatter below the rooms of soft
shoulders. Do you know that
sickness actually sings? Here's the knot of strings you work
at again and again until the paleness
brightens—is it spirit?—is it flesh? *Give me an end to phlegm,*
it rasps, *a pair of hard shoulders, a hat.* The white garlic lesions float
on top, but underneath the color of volcanoes sings
with a weight called *bitterness of god,* because it is so heavy.

My Grandma and the Sack of Potatoes

Though I have no strict record of her
thoughts, just by shaking the potatoes around in a pail
with cold water, blunt blond homely, I can evoke their not sharp

extraordinary fat elbows. *Isn't it lucky we're not a sack of
potatoes?* my grandma Julia says to me one morning, that's one of her
jokes. I don't want to hurt her feelings

but I don't think being potatoes would be so bad—*though not as
contradictory as mine they're also what we
mean by peasant, plain feeling.* And

the potatoes don't fear grandma, even accounting for the way she killed
chickens—*I will never do that,*
she vowed once, but of course later on kills them often because

she's the cook on her farm so it's almost funny
now to imagine her red apron flying up in a squawk-sprint behind
those chickens, a stunning *quick nervous without*

pity, deft quick I am now grabbing your neck.
Afterwards, the disarray!—afterwards
the dizzy North Dakota flat falling, even the horizon prairie far

off lifting up its skirts into a spin! Would the potatoes rather
have been chickens? I tell god I am and am not
joking. They trust her arms even when they're a horror body scrambling

with head cut off in the yard underneath
the clothesline. *If someone had to kill me I would ask her
to.* She must have known there are no drawls in this neck

of the pretty flat grassland since she'd constantly chosen
north, and that the potatoes were meant
to be cherished exactly because they've been born blind,

we think. With what terribly
beautiful ankles, legs and calves did she cross through Iowa, pushing
to go northward across land that

held dangers but was not, for example, Prokofiev's *spark
agonized forever* as if breaking through
the potato bag murmuring *rumble plain, you slice through*

*dark bland juice inside of us, blood
like milk.* I have her brown hair with the tough cowlicks
that I fight. *Stop holding your breath. Lick everything you love,*

don't always let them see you. Though hybrid progeny
of both emigrant Scandinavians and Russian Jews
for example can be *cymbal paschal tornado-toe in the spitting*

locusts' chew as well as *clash! homely dough
of the potato,* what was all the big deal about sex if god
created lightning on top of potato plots and black locusts swarming

underneath thunder? She uses her axe to slay
chickens, but for the potatoes a stubby knife. By their soft
knees I'll also worship them, knocking

on the pillow—with my own palms and knuckles raw *swoosh*
them around in the bucket to take off their baby skins
I mean. Do the sacks of potatoes worry when we are fiends

in the big stove kitchen now about to cook?
Many more of them are also bunched up alongside the infrastructure
of the staircase to the cellar where their eyes blink, not

unhappily, towards the wall. Like many, I have my faces
of *black ice inside the bucket well* as well as *pale
sun on top of the strict cheekbone sheets.* But shouldn't we still cherish

their roving controversial eyes even though they have weak
ears which don't seem to usually explode as ours
do in the microwave rapture of Prokofiev? I want to make more

haystacks in the barn, continually feed the chickens
while learning to wring their necks in addition
to the willful swing cracked in the middle I like to hang my stomach

across. *See those potatoes growing on the prairie
in the flat B minor sections and the afternoon dirt-
ear wind?* She has a lefsa stick for turning potato lefsas on a hot

griddle which even Prokofiev might have opened his raw dark rejoice
mouth for, glowing with Russian
night candles and the huge scary sun. *See that cottonwood*

*air in the splinter shacks, also abandoned
rust-time machinery?* Old potatoes, unlike
the new ones, also like to cleave, fastening onto the upper palette

of the tongue like sticky wafer bread listening to the *fat
phlegm* of the potato groan, you know, that
thud in the left side of the feeling. Do you know,

grandma, I am in a way now sometimes living in the bulgy big
white sack? *I don't think potatoes are*
a nothing. Are they cold before they've been cooked, stolidly

bunched together knocking their knees, lurching together
while they're still intact? Meanwhile, the sack
is pretty silent, it means well—Meanwhile, the sack hurts, *lump bump*

lurch, right here in front
of me next to grandma's multicolored braided round
small rug—for protection it swirls. Then sometimes the potatoes

will say *anything* and *nobody*
seems to mind dancing all out like that to the *cut the rug* Prokofiev,
or the wild piano rag my aunt Alice plays. When anyone says

dumplings require flour and milk not
potatoes, the potatoes scowl. But even in Prokofiev
there is sometimes a *meanwhile*—an *underneath gentle plain*

dough breathe—such as *soup from potatoes is also*
good for flu from viruses. Potatoes press against
each other a lot like the fires on the prairies which I think are smoke

signals since they're visible to everyone for miles—Dirt
can see them god can too probably. *What's the difference*
between potatoes in the dirt and potatoes in the bulgy big white sacks?

Such thin weak fleeces, easily torn—Grandma
planted the eyes she had herself cut
out over the face of the flat prairies, wild, very difficult with family—

Snake

Heavy, getting heavier, I can still hear my fascination with the snake's lack of limbs

and the absence of a
sound which make a kind of crazymaking bleat. *Must be music,*

the faraway farm
voice would say like the opening of a perpetually long unlit muscle which clenches—

then releases—longing

for pasture without unnecessary limbs. *Must be
heaven, my grandma's vegetable*

garden, adds the close voice through which the snake slides dispersed through high

grass bordering on the vegetables. Delighting
in snapping off their stems, from

the very first I made green salads with radishes, onions and tomatoes for lustre

in her garden where the snake ripples

between the soil and the myriad garden plants. The snake of course has skins
upon skins, while my grandma's hair was

sometimes almost lavender sometimes almost green depending

on the weekly drugstore supply of rinses. In those days I'd hear her gravel-tin
   voice beneath
once long cropped-off hair, waving

wildly into semi-
permanent curls—Or garlanding no pleasure by which to redeem the snake, there's her invisible

knob of bun which snakes also go
towards fascinated. In those

days I was sometimes a sieve through which the vessel passed since the snake is what I do not

know—Or *shoulders soft enough, territory lost*

then gained
unexpectedly might also mean intimacy

of relationships, semi-circular, loopy in the noon-time hot place where she picks them up

by their middle from
the long summer grass. So what

if the garden snakes are green? Sometimes she had pale green lights in her white and gray

hair, the white lets them show more. Some
snakes can also be found hanging from the rafters in the cool, mice-barn dark—
   Is the fear

of snakes based on their birth or their feeding

all at once on a whole lump of mouse? What are they doing with that high hump-rise over
there underneath

the barnyard fence—or outside her garden where

we'd run to trip ourselves through green-blue flowerets on top of flax
   suggesting what is

grown outside of accultivated
walls? So what if the desert

snakes are red with diamonds on top of black and white ivory? *Stop*

making my disobedience a duty!, I'd say putting my white hand up to the sky. I'd say
   this when,

first finding my heart
forking in my own body, I'd twist myself away from

the snake as a tumultuous lack of long hair growing into a heavy, curly bun
   and my earlier

reluctance which I hope will keep coming more
and more apart—undoing

itself—since I still don't often know how else to understand

a thing. *Must be heaven,* the quick
garden snake insists coming loaded down with its flesh upon flesh since the desert

snake has ecstasy

but my grandma's garden snakes have
nerve—*What's all this neck*

about? asks the close voice through which the snake still glides—

Absolute Gravity, Time, the Clarinet

When I want to start to breathe
better my grandma starts puffing on her short short cigars—*Sing higher,*

she'll mention
since air is being pressed out of almost

    everything, the clouds, their loud
    sound *scuttering*—I am in my house—Though Stephen

Hawking insists that after the universe's collapse time won't get to start

reversing itself after
all so we won't get to see lightning

before we smell it black ions colliding with summer locust silt

    backwards—My grandma's breathing on her short

cigars—Though clouds keep dropping, the barometric

    pressure is low. But the clarinet playing "Up the Lazy
River" on the radio is sounding pleased

since it's being touched with so much passion
sympathy *as if this music,* it says, *is also not without a skin*—And won't *after all*

    start to grow younger
    backwards toward our

youth, Hawking adds, sounding a little sad as if *lightning thunder*
crack on top of everything might be

losing its
original dirt. The black hole is

a singularity—I almost couldn't catch my breath hearing, on the other side

of the door, that hole breathing in this

music of the clarinet which itself looks something like a lit cigar

or a swarm of locusts against some clouds. *Even the yeast absence of years?* interrupts

the hole with its absence
sound—*Or chords,*

my grandma says referring to radiation which might after all be

escaping as we
speak from the hole out of the very hand

of whom? Or hunger,

I add, feeling this will say
something about my breath—Or is the hole also sometimes trying to escape

from even its *bone*
apart from bone, I want to pick you clean

in the mildew cellar? This is at the bottom of my house on *this* side

of the event horizon of which it is
said *who enters here, abandon*

all hope—But my grandma is puffing on her short short cigars. And especially
since the black

        hole also has
        a temperature, "Up

the Lazy River" may be perfectly made for the clarinet, *especially the further*

and further out you go, she insists through her clouds of cigar smoke

which physicists now think
might be somewhat elastic in that breach because

look,
I said, beginning to breathe

        somewhat deeper, *the escape of radiation makes*
        the singularity less black, though time in there is supposed to be very long, though

her black short cigars are also smoking fiercely—

Of Gravity, Menses, Tomatoes

Because soon the wood
with the smell of rats and tomatoes on top of it will smoke up, meaning

it's almost autumn, I asked the tomatoes *is plenitude a way to*

think? To many tomato mouths, I mean, I've mentioned I've always liked
the ache, where the loose skirts if they're not

trying to be guarded, boil swirl. *Or else fireworks,* that slowing down gravity motion
of the shiny

tomato getting peeled, also often looking for
a mother. Jesus blessed the tomatoes but did

not bleed regularly on top of
the dirt. He's not a mother. I think that some calmness had been planted

into the dirt, *since here,* said the tomatoes, *clothes are not crucial, black*

sky, begetting of children, June bug
phizz. Was the tomato the Versailles of my grandma's vegetables by which we

distinguish *lettuce, worm, potato, beet, faery stem of pea, energetic wild onions?* Imminent,
bold, its meat sucked inside

out sometimes by the low creekside manure bugs though not at first by dirt, are
the tomatoes heavier

when the blood first starts? Blood loves

gravity while I think Jesus' ache pushes him seriously skyward as if falling up out
of the flesh of the breath

inside my grandma's barnyard corral. *They are not the same thing,* I said,

showing him all the sheets with my period stains on them—*you are a
   texture*—thinking
I heard the blood at first *cough cough* where

the thickening was falling out toward my legs. The blood
says *who was really listening to the knees by which tomatoes*

get made? The farm said *who picked them? Is plenitude*

a way to think about bleeding? I then asked the blood itself which seems not
   languid, happy to be
real. I asked god *can you feel*

the lightning juice in the summer red
scream split when the wild June bugs dive? But it seemed god

couldn't. Tomatoes in it howled. Or, opening to blood coming out regularly
   and especially where the flat nights

are black patches
through which the beautiful tomatoes gleam smoke with flourish

meaning the tomatoes are ready to be picked, isn't flesh one of the beautiful

remedies? Or hearing the blood
at first *cough cough* where the thickening is falling out

toward the dirt, are
something huge in the autumn *mirror in the blown tufts sparking* almost turning upside

down, since these, in fact, live with gravity as I do?—

32

The White

is where we get hidden though not exactly blurred,

the birds would say who'd just come out. Birds would often come out of it
when Coltrane played *A Love Supreme*. I think a father

would look like

that, I said once, meaning one of god's faces, which says *that white is where we get*

hidden—This is also
boundless, though, on the other side of

the sax. Sometimes I'm in it, sometimes I'm out. Many birds who were out
were enthralled at the words *empurpled,* at *his sax breaks*

white, which is where Coltrane, playing the seasons' throttling
elegant fluster

through the year would say we're able to be seen. He'd aim

his face at god, in fact, as if he's in a stasis
changing, lifting wind with his sax through the leaves

of the walnut tree
outside for a long time—or, as if god's aiming at him saying he was surprised

about the birds pushing themselves out
of the sax, just as he sometimes bruises his

heels on the cement just after he's arrived. *I've been watching your face above
the cabaret floor,* I'd tell him steaming

inside the smoke, thinking
the white, in fact, became Coltrane through the fierce tunnel *down*

up saxophone whoosh. Its damp
tuft feathers are shaking

out! *Why after all wouldn't these change the configuration of the cadence?* Coltrane would then exclaim, as if he were a part of god arguing with

god. Which is when the birds would answer *Autumn is where we reassemble because the piano's making great strides*

underneath
the sax in a cadence which does expose

the face—And why after all wouldn't the birds become more
and more distinct so

that the white of the other side can't hold us? *I want almost nothing*

exclusively
to, I'd say—

Coo Coo Ghost and the Leak

At night in particular I hear the pigeons moving
outside shifting, I imagine, from foot to foot. Cooing *coo*
coo coo all around my bed and the curtains. One morning
a pigeon eyes me through the window, the armpits
of the bird hairless like mine, the feathers pearl,
mauve, gray—pastel tissue of the ghost. That is
what spirit is, I think, extruding bright colors, all
of them bleached out—stricken. What I once thought
heaven was. I move onto my right side and I am
leaking. Here is where I am pale. I move over to my left, here
is where I am more vibrant, flesh waving and massive as
one hundred loaves. So many kinds of leaking! In one
version, years ago, I have instructed myself to be weightless
thin as god sunlight just so I will want less and be without
sin. I have lightened my heavy pelvis, I have banished
my vagina to Siberia, and all my body hairs. In
another version I have investigated the spirit and found
it is death, neither bad nor good. I have eaten, for
example, memory like a wafer and grown pale. The pigeons eat pale
scraps on the ledges of the windows, and where the human body
of the woman leans toward their subtle beauties, further
and further out—

Jesus and the Gray Sacrament

It is almost Easter and Jesus is tired of New York City.
He would like to ascend with his triangular ankles with hollows

where the wings should be. But there's the gray thing in the top part
of the tree, see it? There's the gray thing at the left part

of the heart. Jesus is the piebald muscle leaning against
it. The tree is naked because spring's still

new but the pigeons with their silver underneath mauve
iridescent want a parade. The City

is hard, the gray wants to soften
it. It folds itself into all the hard things and then has regrets. *Just one hard*

thing I can hang onto, something to resist
me, it weeps with its thick lips, hair and temples oozing the idea

of softness. *Moist ineluctable interminable as a nerve,*
say the pigeons, *who can be your hard thing?* I am

slow in the day, the pigeons ribald. But on the corner of Lexington and 28th
the green awning of the deli the gray is wrestling

has just given way. The confession of the pigeon is that
it is not a ghost. The confession of the knife is that it may possibly succumb

to the gray—it's wailing *be some kind of heaven for me, let me slice*
through. But in the strained city of cathedral

36

lights, I have to glide inbetween thicknesses
to peer out. *Childless,* grayness yells. *Married to the invisible inside*

human, grayness bellows. Of the two graynesses, one is a fat cloak and
veils, the other an inside a whale *lightness*

something. A damp heart in the two barges whistles
at the quay, and the sidewalks whose own ears are the soft soft Jesus

are *too* soft. Meanwhile Jesus is rambunctious
and awkward. He was fooling around with the percussive instruments,

cymbals, deep piano, drums, just as the day shoved out
the sun from its direct hammock place which right now looks as if it's not

smoking its intimidating cigar. Partly veiled in the thickness which
the gray has already kissed, the pigeons like it that I look like them. But it is almost

Easter and Jesus would like to ascend
with the ankles with hollows where the wings should be. If only

the ankles, knees and navel could again split air,
endlessly, as flying requires! Days earlier the sun seemed to be wheels

within wheels, smoking, a good sign. Taking off its
sunglasses. Tipping its tall hat fierceness. Days earlier Jesus was not

pondering triangulating the heavens with his ankles,
the most ticklish part of his foot. Is Jesus'

idea of flying a new joke? Hilarity, in fact, is sometimes a wound he's
been reaching towards. Only *days fertile clouds*

earlier, the sun seemed to be a carousel with bells.
Only *days pewter cups* earlier, bells, grappling the gray, broke

through. Pigeons, ribald. On the sidewalk
I find a medieval *reflect a little bit* penny. Through tiny holes

in the air which the sun presses through, pigeons are flying next to mote-
like creatures grunting *imagine!* marveling at the efficacy

of the wounds chiming through the thick fields of matins ambling
into vespers. *Just one hard thing I can hang onto,*

the grayness weeps, kissing everything with its mouth—Though he knows
the sun is only one kind of heaven, Jesus reconsiders

the feet. In heaven or the *up there* doesn't everything bloom apart
from gray? Don't you feel a need to rise? There's

another woman coming out of the subway over there who looks
like him, no, he looks like her because *bells pewter*

whales later isn't the grayness melting clean through the furrows in almost every
body's tongue going to be accomplished

for awhile? Meanwhile, if he leans
a little further away from it—*forward*—Or, if only he could rise—

Meanwhile, he thinks he sees some kind of gray strings
attached at the very top of the fleece, the flesh body of the gray, he wishes he could—

When the Devoted Rats Come to Hide Themselves in My Breasts

Unbuttoning my black coat buttons for
example then my plaid blouse buttons to let the demanding rats in

I grow heavier (such a wild ride!) though

today through midtown at rush hour the red
    lights and mad cab driver's kaleidoscopically-

veering brakes are *stop*

    and *start* with
    me and so many taxi signs illuminate *available* I could've even caught
more

    though the *forwards*
and the *backwards* make me

nauseous remembering, as I speak, Sarah the cat sniffing my old Mexican pillow
    carefree as can be

forgetting *feathers of the original!* or my excited stomach last week on the way
to Washington Square or for a minute

there on the radio, dead
    air swallowing up the announcer's

remarks—*you only received*
them, he said sadly afterwards to his

guest. Though the cab drivers careening off the curbs of the world

        are not the same thing as the rats
        inside my shirt who prefer trotting

beside the wheels, I mean the ground's spontaneous firm-

feeling *thrum,* to the taxi's erratic
        grind swoon lurch where for some moments now with its *crack low*

ceiling its *rush grunt*
        seats with almost none of its springs

        intact its *creak scream skid* on Fifth Avenue swerving my

flying up throat (I almost hate to tell you this since now you'll know

how many of me there
are) I've been feeling

        again their delicate, scrupulous teeth (I am saying this to prepare you)—the taxis
            careening off
the curbs of the City are not

the same thing as the ground inside my blouse

which knows *fur claws*

in its season, or, *at a point*
at which opposite prongs can join, rats are very convenient. Though

        I sometimes find their devotion

alarming as the one who yearns for a house with *all the female* bleached out
        discovers on finding himself

surrounded by rats, the very house he once coveted—

The Pigeons Have Decided Not to Wound the Sidewalks

And so almost every night you wanted to fall. The fog here

slips in gently between the cracks up nineteen
flights of windows even

the pigeons won't usually come to, it's too high. I think no one believes sadness
   is human

but a disfigurement of the fog. The fog neither rose
nor fell. The way you slip your body in–

between the gray sheets you think
belong to somebody else, perhaps the fascists who make a virtue out of

stopping, tongue in groove, tongue
in groove, heels dug

in and still your eyes are called to that window of next things the way almost
   everything
sometimes wants to fall

at 12:30 a.m., especially, when the City
sky without stars becomes

red and almost every hungry window lights, defying gravity as if falling
were obscene

because there's a texture to absence we still fear. Though

the windows razzledazzle as their reflections glisten past like a cheerleader rooting you on, *empty,*

they encourage,
stammering of sheer

glass, and on the way down the roof of your mouth so bare, harp

bare, pianoforte without strings as if memory of sunrise pricking its fingers above the mountain will have to be

all the music
until you land. I think no

one believes sadness is human but a disfigurement of the dirt. The pigeons have decided not

to wound the sidewalks
with another idea of life

since the world seeds itself down here.

The Different Smokes on Top of the Roof

Just because you have grief doesn't mean
you're not happy, sitting by the big window watching white

smoke curl into the iris above the next door
roof. *Pale blue sponge light taking everything in,* that's why

we've called you god. Though I sometimes also
thought you were a factory—smoke—or a wavy invisible heat. Especially

because smoke has beautiful unobvious
corners and looks like wind made tangible so

I got to see how it tangles and spills over itself and every ending,
I thought, was graceful. If fire could exactly catch

the wind and agree to let itself disperse like that I would have also thought
it was you, *whisper of white*

soot and rusty bilge—sometimes warm as fur—scary ascension
of factory exhaust. So when the grief comes up

again I think first I'll take the poison out of the sky,
then I'll take the poison out of the smoke wanting not to sink like

the concrete ball cut from the crane through the inevitable
sidewalks. The smoke as usual blurts

no, but the sky and especially the birds through it barely even blink
saying *oh everything—invention—sharp edges*

between the wings, and the currents are *yes January kid* and even
a rusty key in the old problem lock of

smog. Because wrestling makes a blue devoted
pigeon and directly cleans the air. So I am both changing

the curious poison as I speak and wondering if it's god's, if he put it there.

Spring at the Cafe Figaro

I

Perhaps not knowing where to begin is a place to

enter from, she says, walking into the Cafe Figaro. Though spring with its green-

awning flutterings and immense-shaped

rooftops has stepped back a foot. Backwards or
      forwards, she thinks, hugging herself because it is again

    somewhat cold. Spring
with its roving *hurry*

      up slow down snap

    up poof as if the meaning of afternoon light in April
were evaporation. Or the *catch*

    catch me of the new butterflies insects moths she has not yet had time

to see, skids across the steep
      roof of the sun's afternoon slant—the atmosphere hugs

    its bell-shaped
curves of air. Or the *wait*

with me, wait with me slowly of the plump
      pigeons, the warm-blooded—how do they get enough

food to live on, how do they stay so plump? Imagining worms or bits of cast-off
bread from the city restaurants and kitchens—Imagining

refuse thrown out
    into the East River near where she lives and

thickening. The river seen from her window is a gray boil

    so that even with all these weather changes there's still lightning

    inside the damp. *Wait with me for what?*

2

Outside the cafe they've started bringing in the metal bridge
chairs and linoleum tables they'd started putting

    out, where

wind starts, as if artlessly
    gracefully spiraling up dust near

    the *where they had been before.* And white graffiti patter

on the brown door across the street puffs its windy chest

    out. It seems to gleam brighter like white iridescent tapeworms

or childhood Ipana toothpaste,
    or the lit night

runs of the grunion along
the edge of the California coasts she has always meant to watch. The way

      in the third from the
      bottom window of the old brick building across the street a cheap

flowered curtain billows
      out *intimacy* on MacDougal Street—left to the imagination, it's all

the invisible gestures *behind*
which the glamour of the curtain keeps

      flaring out, isn't it? Though

there's also its *speak back to me,* the gray clouds which contrary

to sight still move, their
      motion, she thinks, spilling

some of her diet coke, the backlashing
of spring, the breaking, spring putting on a turtleneck as if it were a kind

      of cocky accordion adoration so that where the pleats fold

      in there is sound—so that where the pleats rush out there's the *whoosh*

      of the soundless
      riverboats moving on top of the underwater gray rocky boil

and above them the clouds'
      apparently noiseless *gray float waft*. Like the sound on the other side

of music. Before the invisible,

chasmed splits it
out, or the warp bulge inside air. And does that splitting

hurt? she wonders while, motioning over the waitress, she feels it

pressing against her
open palms as if almost nothing gets moored. *Sad ghost,*

she'll say, finding the only other visible writer in the cafe
today watching

    her, then change her mind watching devotion fold his head back down
again, crack

    by crack. While a new
customer comes

in as a piece of paper outside gets blown, skittering
    across Bleecker Street busy with its *confetti rush motion noise.* Trucks start

honking as if announcing arrival? Departure?

    Or not exactly either since right now there's no other spring

    than this one to catch them, she thinks. While a woman walking past cradles
irises wrapped in a cone

of tissue. While a man outside grinds the butt of his cigarette beneath
    his heel before

    continuing. And there are other
reasons to argue with the direction

of the sun, such as those pieces of paper still being scattered pellmell

by the cold spring breeze, slapping their bellies up against the crumpled *thrown*

> *away already*
in the trashcan, which says of them *far away on the outskirts,*

> *not vague, alien*—Or another

place from which to enter was
perhaps the deepening wrinkle in our foreheads: the condition

> of the body by which the clenched muscle in the neck creases out

while continuing to knead
in unextraordinary

pain absorbed into such motions as lifting the spoon of soup

toward *when did this sizzle-*

> *split start, still burning*
> *soup to the mouth?*—The scalding of the *hot slippery ticklish* of

overcooked brown
onions—Or the now outside

> prick of light spring rain which gets absorbed

into the air around the rusting fire hydrant on the curb
> which is not yesterday's hydrant since time likes to keep swallowing its own

self up. And does *that* swallowing hurt?

she wonders into the hours minutes
> mouthfuls in which the *catch*

catch me of all motions she's not had time to catch spray

down—in a fountain—against
the fat, belled curves of air where the sun still glides its

passionate *forwards and*

back against the pain implicit in neck bones pressing against
muscles. And almost shining—*flicker*—*glisten*—*prick*—isn't this

what we're inside wrestling? Or now
taking off her sweater, does the sun stepping forward

recapture something
hugging her with its *now it's*

warmer than it was
before, now it's more violently cool? Or spring's mysterious roofs *hurry*

up slow down flutter—*flutter*—as if the meaning

of afternoon light in April is now

rain with evaporation, spring with its wobbly ankles, its

fireworks—Spring with its ominous-shaped trowel—

The Rats and the Dirt

As soon as I left, I didn't tell my renter that once the cat

and I had gone the rats intended to skirt the livingroom floor with authority as
    well as the entire nest and bosom

of the house. Everyone knows rats
    love dirt, they love their mother. Baby

rats and adult rats, when the helicopters fly and whirr their blades, cluck *no*

no no because the coldness and
extreme curvature of their limbs

    won't let them likewise negotiate air. Rat

dropping, warm seed, you clod among clods,
I was embarrassed to admit I sometimes think more lucidly

    around noise as well as dirt. Once I came back to the City I knew the rats
back home scrabbling with the iciest,

tiny claws would immediately start looking for heat
because their extremities

    are always cold. Though they won't stop shivering

when one of them has been killed, to themselves and the lice and the smaller
    creatures encountered and to the dirt they'll rasp

dust hair, forest
    dark, I've lived in the safety

of your—Let the spores, the specific, vivid personal dirt motes—and might

add *which thicken the living and make us more*—Once I came back

to the City I also felt like a mote
    with my arms tucked almost all

the way underneath me, not exactly like the rats but a little bit in sympathy
    with their contradictory desires because

    the presence of dirt makes us more
seen—As with my apartment where

the dirt immediately floods to the outside of the big window, pressing to be

    let in and accumulating into *big*
City, you hold me inside your velocity mixed with compression, which

    doesn't let in too much of
the past

nor too much of
    the future

    because the major anthem of this City is still
jazz. I use it to try to anchor

    myself on the nineteenth floor much as the rats who

use dirt and murmur we pledge to get
    dirtier, even if it means penetration

of the air. Meaning if they can they will rise as high as the penthouse in order
    to make more

        dirt. My visible apartment makes
dirt. Dirt makes

        dirt. And to the renter
back in Taos who said there were rat droppings behind my

refrigerator and one dead rat found in the drying
machine, I have not yet told him

the mouse underneath my upstairs queen bed, because though it is *vermin*

        it is not really *rat*. Up here
        the sky, invisible white *whoosh* of heaven, you also

make dirt. *One woman's mouse*

is another man's rat, she said. She said *when you pick them up, their tiny rat*

        belly swells out like a breast. As I
age I plan to get dirtier along with the rats, I plan in fact to bathe

with dirt and have

a look at the tracks where the rat whiskers start, series of imprecise holes. Like
    the home under my nails

in which dirt still loves

        to abide. My grandmother spent her childhood thinking
in a small home made of *dirt*

called sod, and Jesus pushed his fingernails like pencils

through the dust on top of the dirt while he was thinking *visible,* while he
 was thinking *think.* She thought *beware*

of the absence
of rats. Beware of people in nonrat—While

 in the windows of daytime some looked through the holes and saw rats, and in the windows of nighttime some looked

through the holes and saw women (even mistaking
confessions of love for the cool absence

 of sod) *though I sometimes also*

thought my rage toward the perfectly clean was dirty, she confessed—

Spring at the Cafe Figaro 2

I

Sitting again at the corner
table in the Cafe Figaro where MacDougal Street meets

windy Bleecker, just exactly where
    winter gets mitered into spring, she is

managing—how? Feeling safe and aroused by the view of spring seen from this

    particular window? Or the sun which is right now traveling

underneath the skin? Feeling the bottom
of the shoes where the soles spring?—Or in another

direction, spring is my body to which the wind bows down some? To which
    the sounds
        bow down? Inside

her apartment hours earlier, the cat
on the rug lets the purring

sun adore in order to saturate
    her fur which it vibrates then leaves in a textural suddenness *hush!* The cat

    doesn't even blink. The cat seems to swap experiences so easily. You
don't even see

her mouth water at the sun's blast intensity, or
    pucker at its sudden loss *breath across the blossom*

snap—Managing spring *how?* Not knowing where

to begin is also another place from
which to enter? Or the waiter still not noticing her?—when he looks he sees

perhaps only my sharp black eyebrows,

she thinks, my scuffed black shoes—Why does she feel still ghost-

like even though it's
spring? Managing *how?* By choosing a

direction, she hazards, rounding a corner like that taxi into the gusting

raw spring
wind, which just now is scattering blossoms loosed away

from their trees? The pink blossoms could be rice! And she doesn't see

their trees, which at this moment could be invisible apple,
plum or cherry. *Cherry*—a sound which chimes. Nor does she hear the word *torn*

when the pink blossoms strike
the passersby because, though

the sky today is gray, in it there is still so much
light. Nor does she think the word *boundaries* nearing

eventide. A rich direction: around twilight the dark shoulders of evening first

start to
stand up (toward midnight

they'll glower—toward summer they'll swivel, spiked, hot
and tall). Managing as—

what? Returning to thinking as thin ankles on top of the serious,

dwindling ice on the top of the dark body of the lake she doesn't so far sink
through? How much

energy it takes to completely enter
anything, meaning to love—which she imagines

as her heel and her calf muscles pulling forward, roving in almost

all the directions. So that when the pink blossoms strike the going-

ahead trotting motion of the passersby,
for example—when the low moan from the gray barge

seems to leak—even the grayness
of the April street beneath the exhaust feels

to her like lemon chiffon on top of all the shoulders of all the people passing
by her in a direction

of *yellow-light-sun sound glazed with air*—

2

In this case, at this hour, the air
actually feels randy, three weeks grinding into spring and the afternoon's long silk

scarves. In which the most serious part of this moment

is not exactly its light, seen
from this corner

at which passersby speed along into important degrees *away* from
the cold—in which you can feel ankles and feet lightening in their pantyhose

and socks. And the sun, in a way, is at least two

things: lichen on top of stone, and also paleness darker than a color of
banana windiness

and soot. And this sun
and this wind have not started to itch yet,

have they? And in the April City the creatures you cannot usually

see, like the worms in the small green sacs which force them to be
at first curved—at least

curved—are now also eking themselves out into their very first, straightening line. In

the same way joy seems to at first straighten things out even diving ahead horizontally
into the silk long

scarves of the afternoon
which are additional sounds for

wind-air-sun unfurled, before it starts pushing itself out
again into another kind of direction

where the spring, or new word meanings,

froth together like
whipped up yellow gelatin

and milk. Which,
just after they have widened out then looped she has also seen

fall like the heavy, beautifully-scented

word *pomander,*
a gravity nevertheless

wrapped in yellow silk
and also the meaning of something filling

the air blanket with *dark perfume*
inside spring. Fragrance

*of the coming out
interior!* The way, when the cat has filled herself up on top of someone's

lap and jumps

off suddenly, they might tremble at the scary rungs
of the words *inside* and

out since to lovers direction is crucial, meaning almost everything

there is—*Managing as what?*
Acacias spearing the dirt and sidewalk cracks? How the wind

she thinks at this moment is the most serious thing among all the directions?

Or black walking dress shoes on top of the pavement *clack
clack clack?* She pauses

against the soft
leather

of the wind. It interrupts
her with its flaw of invisibility—the waiter still hasn't

come. The view from this particular

window in the cigarette section is arousing though she doesn't like the
smoke. The wind

with its flaw of erraticism interrupts
her. The wind with its excess flares

of intensity, its *scatter-down* paws. And what could be other

sounds for this afternoon with its sharp soft velvet languor and its
teeth which like to point? And what after all

could be other possible names for the fierce sun-snuffing feelings

inside this gray cloud by which altarboys
put out decades of flame

on top of long gold tapers? Or the up there *ecstasy uncertainty cold*

of the *behind*
the cloudiness blue? Even in this thick

fog dampness above
last night's soft round black and red shoulders

does anyone ever forget the color

sounds behind *gray*
bunting sky? Or how about the wind-cloth with its blind quixotic not telling

    us exactly everything

we want to know? The wind is pretty
mum, she thinks, or discrete. Or

    loud, report
        the thorned horns from the other side of the glass. *With this side of the trellis,*

the sirens urge. *On the other side of the roses,*

add the liquid black motors in
    front of the red *don't walk* light. Idling. Then again revving up.

3

She is still inside
the Cafe Figaro, throwing the black wool coat off her shoulders, next to that

woman's thin cigarette arcing
down from its smoke. At this

point in April the wind is not exactly
    cold, so that when the door to Cafe Figaro opens it will suggest trellises

on their sides, even wheelbarrows, as
much as the scooping

    out *bellow*
of the barge which wants to dock

    or dislodge. And all of their bodies are

talking aren't they, every one making its sounds? Or the cool *coo coo* uninterest
of the pigeons for any kinds

of boundaries since angling

    into different directions *is* what they want, isn't it? She lets the wind interrupt

    her since it's no longer bringing

    in cold. Can you hear it howl? How almost precisely it flings out its whips?

Passersby
bend down their necks a little, up,

down, sideways, then their shoulders into a quince mildness but with the same

    sound of the violin string vibrating next
    to the performer's ear. In the same

way, now, inside the cafe the first version of Eric Clapton's "Layla," beginning
    with a climax

    which shifts into gestures
such as violence, or,

    for example, the kiss, unwinds itself out
    direction

upon direction—In the same

way she senses her own ears quivering *flutter—flutter*

    out—when she looks at the green

flexible awning above the MacDougal Street Cafe waving with a *crack*
    lick, or the sun, or the lemon with dark

perfume inside it swirling dropping

wind—They
 also hold their ears out, like water, testing, then whipping again the chords—

Inside the Cafe Lanterna di Vittorio

Was it the fever of summer or
the flocking up and down of pigeons pushing me inside? What did it

    mean where almost every day was looking

up into the face of gods jammed
inside those upper darknesses in trees, I've been aching with you? *Do you know*

what's hurting you? the pigeons asked, pleased

that so much transparency worn for the sun's
    sake could be shaken off for awhile. But it wasn't as simple as leaving the sax

    in Washington Square Park, squirting

its spotlight up into the bruised
knots of birds. Though sometimes the owner Vittorio would give me iced

coffees on the house not
    unlike the cafe shadows Bach was

moving his neck methodically across, apparently very restless. And sometimes I'd see

    pigeons flock up outside in a suddenness

which made my breasts feel abandoned in the swift opening of Oriental fans,
    it's their instinct. I'd admire

too, Bach's arched palms which fingered the recesses

of the room so
> adroitly. They cut

the strong summer lawns to sift some of the brightness out. While the sun
> broke in with *my enthusiastic raptures, continual*

> *goodbyes* against the cello, no, the oboe of

the slow ceiling fans. I liked feeling his fingers, their coolness fugues—long cool tempers of his fingers. Or the pigeons would ask *do you know*

what's hurting
you? and I'd imagine their irises enlarging

> at the *so much sun with the roses*
> *on it* trembling at the *blinking*

inside the bright trellis ribs. And Bach's hands could have been small even with

> all their precision. And
the softening necks of the customers, what of them?

the pigeons
wheezed, a little bent

over the hot pavement not unlike

> the lavender flowerets on the stalk in the swollen belly of the clear rose

vase. Bach's hands

after all had been fingering darknesses we didn't completely know

> the names to but felt raised up on our flesh
> as goosebumps,

hairs—The pigeons are pleased that so much transparency worn for the sun's

sake can be shaken off
    for awhile. *The faces of lovers have disappeared between our legs for days,*

    shadows pressed
back, *until the dogs start barking,*

the customers begin to leave
    and the pigeons hold up hasty mirrors to their mouths arguing it's time to start

    recircling—Dark of

summer, I'd
interrupt, *you have that long white*

    neck, I've been watching
    you bend it down over my table of coffee in the Cafe Lanterna di Vittorio—

Kissing the Flame and Yellow Tulips

When the flame and yellow tulips
begin dying in the air on top
of the coffee table, I move across the room to kiss
their insides. They're completely
opened today bending over
their own shoulders, the rim
of my grandmother's cut glass vase,
and I'm thinking a thing becomes its death—
that beauty goes past
itself into its finishing with such force
it seems to come from nowhere straining

to end. Jesus you
loved the lilies of the valley didn't you?—their
bright heads blown between worlds not
considering their rapture. Nor
did I always slash my arguments
into your parable, I wanted to be
the lilies slanting,
my mouth straight into the rain which knows
my name . . . You leave
the valley of the lilies suffused with their days of glory,

intact, telling
us their sheen will rapture through the
color which wind and rain don't
break. Harder to believe
you now, hill against which the deep red tongues of
the tulips splay—bend

down your head a little, they have crucial
mouths. And for a while

when I said a thing is only
its death, their milk teeth bruised me at the tongue
because they insist a thing is its own every
day and after dark un–
folding. When I return to the tulips one
gorgeous day before their death, they almost won't let
me, they're flame-
colored lips barely entering the mind after
all they hugely explain—

Quartet for Three Instruments

It is summer, and the rats in my house are, apparently,

shedding. Even baby ratlets shed. Jesus is up again—his
sandal thongs purple. I remember,

> lately, hearing the percussiveness
> of jazz. I asked *Did someone give you a haircut? Summer*

cuts us, the rats answered, dropping their voice
down to a little *wine staccato goblet* so that even

the just on the other side spring can't

hear them. The summer sky, not sheltering like the membrane on
the inside of the womb, is turning into *gorgeous*

mouth of wine or else the thick outside

> *lanolin of fur*—at least into the *staccato legato*
> *heart* which might be the heaven on this side

of Charlie Parker's horn. Jesus is out
again—the clouds thong purple—I remember

> lately hearing the obsessiveness of the strings. While

the rats are back on top of the cedar crawlspaces and
closets underneath the vigas the way I think summer is still

backing out of spring, dancing with especial
fervor since for months now the reluctant

        renter has been gone. Spring
        is gone. I remember also hearing the percussiveness

of the rats just as Jesus might have still thought *inside
the bowels of the earth* was not intense

        enough for the howl on the second day of the passion. *Or*

        the cutting, the rats still say, big chunks
        of fur falling down where Charlie Parker's

mouth and fingers hurt—They say *fur of the falling
down is summer.* I say *heat of*

        summer is the howl. Or the season perhaps passes as
        horns we may not feel except as cutting with a little *rat*

italic lanolin emphasis, the humpy

purple ending of the week. Though I have in fact never
        touched them, their bellies are splaying a touch

        off-key just as Charlie Parker's tenor sax playing gorgeous

lopsided wasn't able to mask his
infatuated hands. And when he sings his torn

heart turns for awhile,
        up, and for awhile the shaved rat bellies will almost be

too pink. I think also the summer
thunderstorms will prick them, I think also it is good for *heat*

of summer not to spurt out only in a line
since, though I have never actually touched

    them, their summer bellies are *soft grapes*
    beneath our feet until the cooling of Charlie Parker's fingers—

The Tulip Sacrament

Over there is the vase, the sticky
sky—over here the lump, gray wet matter the tulips like
to break through. I have been thinking
maybe god cuts us all off
at the stalk and sends us down to be born so he
can watch us. As I watch the tulips. For him in the watching
what glory and what grief, as he is compelled
as I am to
keep observing. Each time he becomes terribly

attached. Please don't say the words
terrible beauty, god. Each time it is beauty
which is arresting him, our happiness,
and the sad fact that the tulips have
been cut and he
knows it. God is patient with
the guilt, just as we are. Just ask my cat Sarah who lifts
up her eyes. What are you looking at? Is it the sun
which is a tender and hard soft spot
today all at the same
time? She continues to smile. The still
bright leaves of
the tulips remind me of green butter,
clear pungence, glee. I am surprised the other
day when someone tells me I have faith because I know
for a fact I have left everything I had
to have faith for

꽃

Always looking
for the form, like a lover, a mad lover,

the bones, here is my faith: the tulips are the same thing as Prokofiev's
Third Piano Concerto which says *belong to
no one*—The italics are the wet
pursed lips of the jazz which
says *here's
your today. Gray joy. Bright
moodiness. Here is trembling. Here is spring
sleet.* Prokofiev's
performance of his own *Third Piano Concerto* is more wobbly
than any other version of his music
I have ever heard. The castanettes
are sharper. The crisis
more intense. Here's my
faith but I have put faith from me. At
the same time that Prokofiev at the piano is pulling inside
through his own thickness—(hear it slow-
    er—*thickness*)—a woman is
saying *the tulips are craft but when
you leave them alone they become their presence.* I didn't
get it. I think she meant by craft, sometimes,
the bones. I said *the tulips are
presence to me when I kiss them, just as
they are presence when I am walking
away.* I think she meant perhaps what the wind
just brought in. For example the sour
purple smell of the old Lutheran aisles and their pews. I will never
forget that second
    smell of god, not if I die tomorrow. Will the sour smell
argue with the tulips, their crucial texts, their
right to exist?

༄

What did she mean
about the tulips? It made me feel slow and that the actual dark

shape of the air was pressing against me. My heart
brrrred with the lips. With Prokofiev's
fingers on top of the keys, no, under-
neath inside
—there—julep
vapor where I think I'll hurt and won't hurt
you. What's the difference between the metaphor
and the story? Why couldn't the tulips
and their presence live together? Sing, then
conjoin? I put
my neck next to her neck,
vibrating, a little strict. A man thinks the most emotional
music will endure, he
says *don't worry, if it's too emotional time fades*
it until it's exactly emotional
enough. The rest of the *much*
of the honey
sticks. Does the craft mean

the art, dear witches? The craft, perhaps the bones
lifted up, away from these wings? We know
this music as if we had been born into it, it can't be
controlled. And why wouldn't the craft of the tulips have
married their presence for all time and forever
until death do us part?

❧

This morning I assume craft doesn't mean perfection
death, the end, though it sometimes includes
waiting. Is the craft
of mornings these tulips blistering the air? The air just
waking up? The air perplexed? The air
quiet? The tulips will now open further

as the sun strikes bells at their
mouths. I mean, while being yanks
their glister open. The air somewhat
> injured. And the gold
worms of language! I think meanings love
the sun which hurries their opening hours
along and so expedites their
death. The air a little assaulted (well, it hurries
in a way). The sun and the tulips tango-
ing, perhaps anything that brings us
closer to our
death is an assault. Or maybe it's

craft. Listen. Prokofiev assaults
the wound, the very salt essence
of the prayer. This gives the not uniform bright and
the dark spirit form. Is the sun
an assault? a rapture? The sun
requires for our happiness that we
be intense, I mean honest, not in a bad
way. It is the function of time now to take ourselves
seriously. That is why
the roots of the tulips and the lilacs have been
cut. Automatically, in a way, the cutting cuts out some
laziness, drift. In case we had thought
we would put off
loving ourselves. In case we had
thought we would live forever. Lovers,
listen: just like the tulips we are in
the craft
of the moment of the gray sky *and* the tulips of the passing morning . . .

ʄʘ

So afraid of being left for any reason I have kept on being
left. That is why I fear
so much my own white wormlets, don't corrupt
my womb. Or I have myself kept
on leaving, the tulips, the flesh leaning out
towards the *towards*. Today I have set between you
two green sticks of candle, see? Dark
green. What I want to know exactly is how you *do*
love, god. Do you feel as we do all the blood between
these *italics?* The tulips do their simplest *arpeggios* to
roughly balance
everything. Is there a craft
of the fear, whirling out or inside
it? I feared the splitting
tongue which that church swore twisted
out of your throat so it hung
swollen, also loose. Not
bone. Split
red. Not torn. It is the morning of Prokofiev and

A Mighty Fortress Is Our God which Mendelssohn embellished,
no, widened out of what Bach's
    invention had originally
torn. He had to, he had missed and longed for the fortress,
which is a dark and purplish
squarish rectangle. It changes shape. Supple. Not
squat. What you fear
you will become. That is why Esther became
queen and rushed straight
on into her husband's gold death sceptre to save Israel
saying that the bottom of her skirt was jaundiced,
pumice,
somewhat pale. That the bottoms

of her own feet were very tender, not
random, able to be torn. She said what you fear
you will become
and jumped

into the craft of
the moment the way the word becomes living
skin. Touch your own brown arm,
there, where the flesh is freckled. I understand
the violin's throbbing,
wailing
because it is afraid that god or *god's*
love will not eat it. It is running
to catch up. Or *god's purple gentian attention,*
my little gold . . . are you hungry? Please
eat. Will my fear
make you abandon me? Don't
please. Are you god
     the lump? the bored?
the substance I can't stop? I was going to say I can't forgive
you, but I think I can. There's
dirt, I do.

University Press of New England publishes books under its own imprint and is the publisher for Brandeis University Press, Dartmouth College, Middlebury College Press, University of New Hampshire, University of Rhode Island, Tufts University, University of Vermont, Wesleyan University Press, and Salzburg Seminar.

About the Author
'Annah Sobelman was born in Los Angeles and has since lived in New York City, and the Sangre de Cristo Mountains of Taos, New Mexico, where she makes her home. Her poems have appeared in such periodicals as *The Antioch Review, The Appalachee Quarterly, The Denver Quarterly, Poetry/L.A., The Santa Fe Literary Review,* and others. She is a graduate of University of Southern California, Pepperdine Law School, New York University School of Law, and the University of Iowa Writer's Workshop, and has edited and published *The Taos Review.*

Library of Congress Cataloging-in-Publication Data
Sobelman, 'Annah.
    The tulip sacrament : poems / by 'Annah Sobelman.
      p. cm. — (Wesleyan poetry)
      ISBN 0-8195-2223-6 (cl). — ISBN 0-8195-1227-3 (pa)
      I. Title. II. Series.
PS3569.025T85 1995
811'.54—dc20   94-48729

∞